D1383784

Elias Hill

Self-published, Tiny Camel Books
More 101 So Bad, They're Good Dad Jokes

Tiny Camel Books
tinycamelbooks.com
tinycamelbooks@gmail.com

More 101 So Bad, They're Good Dad Jokes

By: Elias Hill

Illustrations By: Katherine Hogan

Dad, I heard you were voted dentist of the year!

Yes, they gave me a little plaque.

There are three kinds of people in the world...

those who are good at math and those who aren't.

Dad do you like cats?

Yes, it's just that I can't eat a whole one by myself.

i before e,
except after c
That's weird.

Dad, I think life gave me melons.
Maybe you're dyslexic.

Dad, there's a frog parked in front of the house.

Good, all others will be toad.

Which former president is the least guilty?
Lincoln.
He’s in a cent.

If you wait long enough to make dinner...

everyone will just eat cereal. It's science.

So what if I don't know what "Armageddon" means.
It's not like it's the end of the world.

Dad where did you find gas for 99 cents?
At the burrito place.

Dad, why won't you tell me the joke about the roof?
Because it's way over your head, son.

I don't do this very often, but could I interest you in a date?

Dad, can I watch the TV?
Sure, just don't turn it on.

Dad, what's your favorite bird?

A peacock because they pay attention to de-tail!

I got you a comb for your birthdday.
Great, I'll never part with it.

Always be nice to clones.
They're people two.

I bought some shoes from a guy on the street.

I don't know what he laced them with, but I've been tripping all day!

Dad, which state has the smallest drinks?
Mini-soda!

I wondered why the volleyball was getting bigger.
Then it hit me.

Dad, why do moon rocks taste better than earth rocks?
They're meteor.

Dad, why do you keep moving away from those trees?

They just look shady to me.

I quite my job at the coffee shop.
Day after day, some old grind.

Dad, what's middle age?
When your age starts showing around your middle.

Dad, why do men usually die before their wives?
They want to.

Honey, you make my knees weak.

Just kidding, yesterday was leg day at the gym.

Why did the chicken go to the psychic?
To get to the other side!

What did the mountain climber say to his son?
Watch out, Cliff!

Dad, how does a penguin build his house?
Igloos it together.

How do you make a tissue dance?

You put a bunch of boogie in it.

Dad, you have a phone call.
I told you if it's for me, don't answer it!

It's really confusing when sentences don't end
they way you refrigerator.

How many hipsters does it take to screw in a lightbulb?
It's really an obsure number, you've probably never heard of it.

Dad, why was the ocean embarrassed?
Because all the fish could see its bottom.

What did the black bug say as it slid down the zebra?

Now you see me, now you don't. Now you see me, now you don't...

What does a snail say when he's riding a turtle?

Wheeeeeee!

Dad, your name is Toby, how can you say you were named after Abraham Lincoln?

Well I wasn't named BEFORE him!

Dad, why do I
have to the mow
the yard again?

Because I'm a
certified lawn
enforcement
officer!

If these kids are behaving then they're mine.

If not, I'm just an uncle.

Campfires.
They're always fun and games until someone loses a wiener.

Dad, what's trail mix?

Candy with obstacles.

I'm a leader, not a follower.

Unless it's a dark basement. Then you're totally going first.

Dad I thought you were into fitness.
Yeah, fitness whole pizza into my mouth.

Relax.
Take a breath.
And hold it for 30 minutes.

Dad, should I always give 100 percent?
Yes, unless you're donating blood.

Don’t get caulky.

Dad, do you like golf?
I like big putts and I cannot lie.

Remember too much pi
gives you a large circumference.

What did the magician say to the fisherman?
Pick a cod, any cod.

Root beer.

Dad, my teacher's eyes were crossed today.
Sounds like she couldn't control her pupils.

What did one eye say to the other?

Don't look now but something between us smells.

Why can't I yell through the screen?
Because you'll strain your voice.

Why don't you like wearing those hospital robes?
Because I know my end is in sight.

Did you see the documentary on ship buidling?
Yes, it was riveting.

Dad, why do writers constantly feel cold?

Because they're surrounded by drafts.

I told mom she drew her eyebrows on too high.
Did she look surprised?

What's the difference between
a good joke and a bad joke timing.

What do you call a dog that can do magic tricks?

A labracadabrador.

What do you call a Frenchman wearing sandals?
Phillipe Phillope.

Dad, how many opticians does it take to change a lightbulb?

Is it one or two?
One... or two?

Dad, I can teach you how to do the splits. How flexible are you?
Well, I can't make Wednesdays.

No, dad, you can't talk to John he's in jail.

Oh, ok, what's his cell number?

What do cows
have hooves
instead of feet?

Because they
lactose.

What did the cell say to his sister after she stepped on his foot?

Mitosis!

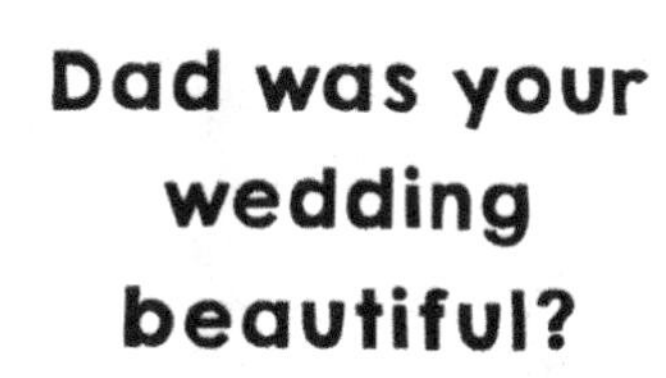

Yes, even the cake was in tiers.

Dad, how do you tell alligators and crocodiles apart?

One will see you later, the other will see you in awhile.

My wife asked for her lipstick but I accidentally gave her a gluestick.

She's still not talking to me.

Here's your check. Can I get you anything else?

Yeah, maybe someone to pay the check!

Why did the can crusher quit his job?
Because it was soda pressing.

I've got a great salt joke.
It's sodium funny.

Mary was a vegetarian too.

But then she had a little lamb.

Dad, what do you want for breakfast?
Omlette you decide.

Dad, here's an underwear joke.
I hope it's brief.

Did you know french fries don't come from France?
They were made in Greece.

Dad are you having fun doing the laundry?
Loads.

Did Einstein get along with his parents?

Relatively speaking.

Dad, what does a lumberjack love most about his laptop?
Logging in.

Someone stole my coffee.
I'm the victim of a mugging.

I just won a blue ribbon for my pumpkin at the state fair!
Oh my gourd!

Never get sick at an airport.
That's a terminal illness.

I once was so poor I couldn't afford electricity.
The darkest days of my life.

People at work were talking behind my back.
They discussed me.

Dad, why do you like mushrooms so much?
Never forget I'm a fungi.

Dad, you ate all the pastries!
Doughnut judge me.

Dad, do you even work out?
I do more deadlifting than a mortician.

What do you get when you cross a joke with a rhetorical question?

Dad, you worked in a prison library?
Yep, it had its prose and cons.

Dad, can we take a trip to see some llamas?

Sure, alpaca my bags.

Dogs can't operate an MRI machine.

But catscan.

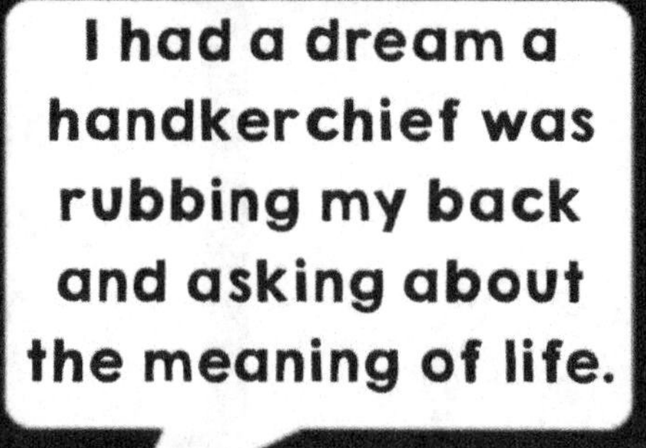

It was a deep tissue massage.

Dad, do you practice yoga to deal with people who bother you?
Yes, I tell them nama-stay over there!

You're living, you occupy space and you have mass. You know what that means?

You matter!

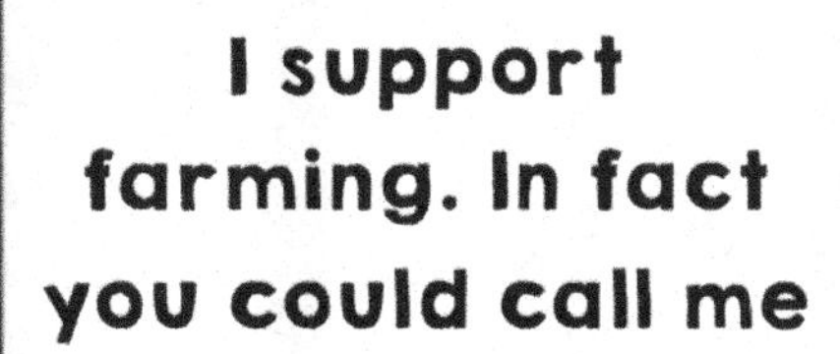
I support farming. In fact you could call me

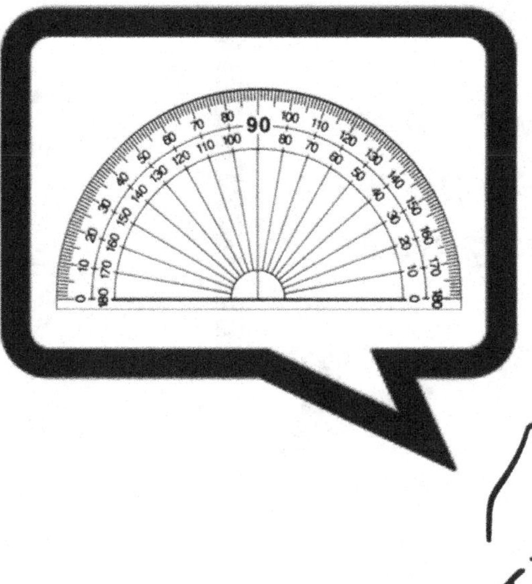

I see you bought owl the cheep eggs.

Oh, bird puns. Toucan play at that game.

Why did grandma stop entering the sewing contests?
She wanted to quilt while she was ahead.

Was that freezing rain outside?
Because it hurt like hail.

I'd wear skinny jeans,
but I could never pull them off.

What's up with that skeleton?

It's just trying tibia a little humerus.

I forgot what it's like at the dentist.
Oh, you know the drill.

Dad, why do you want to be cremated instead of buried?

Because I like to think outside the box.

When does a joke become a dad joke?
When it's fully groan.